T0362610

CONTENTS

3	Architectural Beginnings
7	Introduction
13	Department of Education Building
17	Transport House
19	BMA House
21	City Mutual Life Building
25	Sydney Morning Herald Building
29	Bryant House
33	Commonwealth Bank Building
37	MLC Building
41	Sun Building
43	David Jones Buildings
47	Hyde Park Anzac Memorial
51	Foys Building
55	Plaza Theatre
59	Metropolitan Water, Sewerage & Drainage Board Building
61	Gowings Building
65	Dymocks Building
69	Grace Building
73	AWA Tower
77	Railway House
79	Commercial Banking & Bank of NSW Buildings
83	Sydney Harbour Bridge
86	George Raynor Hoff
88	Timeline
90	Glossary

ARCHITECTURAL BEGINNINGS

When Captain Arthur Phillip sailed into Botany Bay, on the east coast of Australia, in January 1788, he was unimpressed. The bay was unprotected and shallow and surrounded by poor soil and its shore was observed to be unproductive with scarce fresh water. Having led a fleet of ships halfway around the world to found a penal colony for British convicts, he decided to explore further north for a better location.

He found it just 12 kilometres up the coast. Port Jackson was an inlet discovered and named by Captain James Cook in 1770 although it was not extensively explored at the time. What Phillip found as he ventured up the inlet was, in his opinion, 'the finest harbour in the world'.

Named after the British Home Secretary Thomas Townshend (Lord Sydney), Sydney Cove was a well sheltered deep water anchorage with ample fresh water supplies. It was a perfect site for the first official British settlement on the Australian continent.

FOR THE FIRST TWO
DECADES OF SYDNEY'S
EXISTENCE THE COLONY
WAS SO LACKING IN
APPROPRIATE SKILLS
AND TOOLS THAT THE
MAJORITY OF BUILDINGS
CONSTRUCTED WERE
OF POOR QUALITY AND
IN NEED OF CONSTANT
MAINTENANCE.

The situation changed dramatically with the appointment of Major-General Lachlan Macquarie as Governor of New South Wales in 1810. Finding many structures throughout the settlement in a 'most ruinous state of decay', Macquarie implemented a set of building codes that dictated a minimum standard for any future construction. Teaming up with convicted forger and architect Francis Greenway, the Governor also commissioned a series of classically inspired public buildings including Hyde Park Barracks (1819) and St James Church (1824), both of which still stand today.

From the mid to late 19th century architectural trends in Sydney closely followed those adopted throughout the British Empire. Grand classical revival styles were used extensively for public and administrative buildings whilst well to do residents displayed their wealth with elaborate Victorian Italianate or sober Georgian home designs.

INTRODUCTION

The dawn of the 20th century signalled a series of significant changes to the social and urban fabric of Australia. The year 1901 saw the death of Queen Victoria (along with her eponymous 19th century era) after a reign of 63 years, and witnessed the birth of the nation of Australia with the federation of the colonies. Sydney became the capital of the state of New South Wales with a turn of the century population of around 480,000, making it one of the largest cities in the Western world.

Architecturally, styles popular in the late 1800s continued to be utilised for new buildings throughout the city, occasionally incorporating design elements from contemporary trends emerging from Europe such as the Art Nouveau movement. 'Federation' is the umbrella term, coined in 1969, that covers the period from around 1890 to 1915 and encompasses such revival styles as Free Classical, Anglo-Dutch and Queen Anne.

DESPITE FORMING A NEW
NATION AT THE BEGINNING OF
A NEW CENTURY, AS WITH THE
PREVALENT ARCHITECTURAL
STYLES, THERE WAS A
LINGERING DESIRE TO
MAINTAIN STRONG TIES
TO THE OLD WORLD.

Australia felt obliged to maintain the prestige of the British Empire and when war erupted in 1914 Australian sons rushed to defend it. Four years later Europe was in ruins and millions of lives had been lost, including over 60,000 Australians. The war had deeply shocked the nation but its end triggered a building boom to provide housing for returned soldiers and their families. In Sydney a general economic upturn and increasing prosperity in the immediate post-war years also led to major redevelopments and construction in the CBD. In addition to architectural styles such as Art Deco and early Modernism, new building technologies were adopted from the United States enabling the design of taller buildings and apartments.

Although the Great Depression slowed or halted much of this new urban development throughout the 1930s, it also produced one of Sydney's most impressive and recognisable feats of civil engineering, the Sydney Harbour Bridge.

Overall the inter-war years saw the modernisation of Sydney, transforming a low rise 19th century city into an increasingly high rise 20th century metropolis.

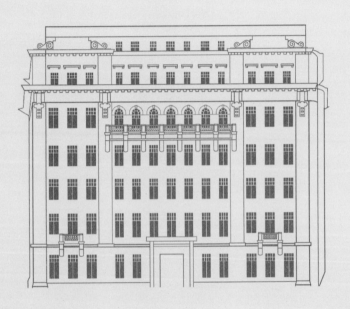

DEPARTMENT OF EDUCATION BUILDING

Occupying an entire city block, the imposing Department of Education Building was one of the last stone-faced structures to be commissioned by the NSW Government. George McRae was a Scottish architect who, having migrated to Australia in 1884, was appointed City Architect in 1889. Over the following years he designed many of Sydney's grandest architectural landmarks including the Queen Victoria Building (1898), becoming New South Wales Government Architect in 1912. McCrae's later projects were primarily designed in the Edwardian Baroque style (later termed Federation Free style), reflecting contemporary architectural fashions in England, and this building is a particularly handsome example.

Sitting on a rusticated sandstone base the first level features articulated quoins and piers. A pattern of symmetrically placed rectangular windows and balcony arrangements is repeated on each elevation with a series of arched openings decorating the upper levels. The top floor is capped with a relatively simple cornice with dentils, above which rises the roof parapet. The Bridge Street facade is entered via a central porch flanked by Doric columns and topped by an ornately decorated broken pediment. The seamless unified appearance of the building belies the fact that it was actually built in two stages. The north section was constructed c1912-14 whilst the southern part was added in 1930.

⭐ OF NOTE

Booth House / 1938 / 44 Bridge Street

Opposite the Department of Education Building, on the corner of Bridge and Young Streets, is the former 'Booth House', named after the original owners Frederick H. Booth & Sons. A fine example of the Late Deco Functionalist style, bands of brick divide large ribbon windows that allow maximum light to penetrate the office spaces. Unusually for a progressive inter-war building, the base is composed of rusticated sandstone.

Although the decorative features and heavy masonry facades recall 19th century architectural styles, the building was constructed using contemporary steel frame and concrete slab methods, demonstrating the emerging technology of the new century.

TRANSPORT HOUSE

Transport House was constructed in order to accommodate the entire Department of Road Transport and Tramways under one roof. Previously its functions had been scattered throughout various CBD locations, and the move reflected similar centralisation activities of various government administrative bodies (such as the Department of Education) to the precinct from the 1850s onwards.

The building is a well preserved example of the Stripped Classical style with Art Deco detailing. The Macquarie Street facade is formed in a classical manner with clearly defined base, colonnade and cornice, all clad in honey coloured sandstone. Rising up four floors, the ten fluted pilasters are grouped in pairs and define the five window bays. Window frames and spandrels are bronze and subtly detailed to emphasise the verticality of the facade. The central entrance is framed in red granite with bronze doors, above which sits a bronze relief of the Greek god Hermes. It is one of the many sculptural details featured on the building designed by artist Rayner Hoff, a WW1 veteran who also designed the sculptures and reliefs for the Hyde Park ANZAC memorial.

Extending across the block, the Phillip Street facade boasts a further three storeys and is designed with more emphasis on the Art Deco style. Flanked by two brick-faced bays, the central recessed facade sits on a simplified base and features seven expressed sandstone fins that are stepped beyond the top level.

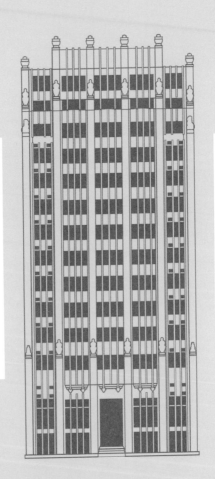

BMA HOUSE

Founded in England in 1832, the British Medical Association was responsible for the promotion and protection of the medical profession and its activities. In 1879 branches were established in Victoria, NSW and Queensland. By the 1920s the NSW branch, under the secretaryship of Dr Robert Todd, was flourishing and lots 17 and 18 in Macquarie Street had been acquired for the proposed construction of a new headquarters.

Rising to 12 storeys the building was designed in the Skyscraper Gothic manner which was popular in the United States at the time. Early examples such as the Woolworth Building in New York (1913) exhibited elements which would become signatures of the style such as soaring vertical forms and cathedral-like detailing. BMA House possesses many of these attributes including a facade clad in glazed terracotta tiles. Referred to as 'faience', tiled finishes were used extensively in American commercial architecture from the 1890s to the 1930s and made popular in Australia by architects such as Harry Norris in Melbourne (The Nicholas Building, 1926).

One of Sydney's tallest buildings at the time, the facade of BMA House is dominated by three central expressed window bays with ornately tiled spandrels and mullions decorated with rope-like mouldings. Various sculptures adorn the building including winged gargoyles hanging above the ground level, four granite lions on the third and a pair of koalas flanking the eleventh. Where the facade steps back at level 12 six knights can be seen crouching behind their shields which display the Rod of Asclepius (associated with medicine and health care).

CITY MUTUAL LIFE BUILDING

From the 1850s onwards, sparked largely by the discovery of gold, Australia's major cities witnessed enormous economic growth. The increased economic activity and associated risks prompted the establishment of numerous insurance companies throughout the late 19th century. Founded in 1878, the City Mutual Life Assurance Company first erected an office building on the Hunter and Bligh Streets corner site in 1893. As the 1930s dawned, having experienced three decades of prosperity, the company decided to rebuild on the site. A design competition was initiated and Emil Sodersten was announced as the winning architect.

Modelled on contemporary American skyscrapers, the City Mutual Building is composed of a steel frame clad in Wondabyne sandstone (from the NSW Central Coast) above a red granite two-storey base. This contrast in cladding materials also highlights the differing window treatments with large bronze-framed glazing used for the ground and first floors and steel framed casement windows above. Designed as six panel units that follow the expressed vertical serrated form of the facade, they lend a unique repetitive textural quality to the surface. Utilising the corner site in dramatic fashion, the central tower structure rises in multiple planes with tall rectangular windows, continuous expressed mullions and decorative finned elements enhancing the verticality. The black granite entrance is decorated with another fine piece by sculptor Rayner Hoff. The copper bas-relief, known as 'The Flight From Vesuvius', depicts a man protecting his family in Pompeii and is flanked by depictions of Australian flora.

When completed in 1936 a contemporary architectural magazine reported that 'the whole of Sydney is talking about the new City Mutual Building... People passing in the trams lean forward to gaze upon it, while those walking up Hunter Street stop to admire its streamlined symmetry'.

Highly original both inside and out, the City Mutual Building remains one of the city's best examples of commercial Art Deco architecture.

SYDNEY MORNING HERALD BUILDING

The Sydney Herald newspaper was founded in 1831 by former employees of the Sydney Gazette which existed from 1803 to 1842. In 1841 the paper was purchased by John Fairfax who renamed it The Sydney Morning Herald. Fairfax, who had arrived in Sydney from England in 1838 with just £5 in his pocket, went on to establish a business empire that survives to this day as Fairfax Media.

The site at the corner of Pitt, Hunter and O'Connell Streets had been home to the paper since 1856, when Fairfax was joined by his son James in the family business. By 1920 the newspaper had outgrown the premises and a new office building was planned for the site. The new headquarters was constructed in three stages from 1924 to 1929 with the 1856 building being used until stage one was completed. The new design reflected the popular Commercial Palazzo style that emerged from the United States during the early 20th century. Less progressive than contemporary Chicago School architecture, Commercial Palazzo utilised modern internal engineering techniques (steel or concrete frames) but continued with classically derived external forms and decoration.

The sandstone building sits on a two-storey base of smooth-faced rusticated trachyte. Above ground level decoration is generally sparse with curved pediments capping the second floor windows and a series of Doric order pilasters adorning levels six to nine.

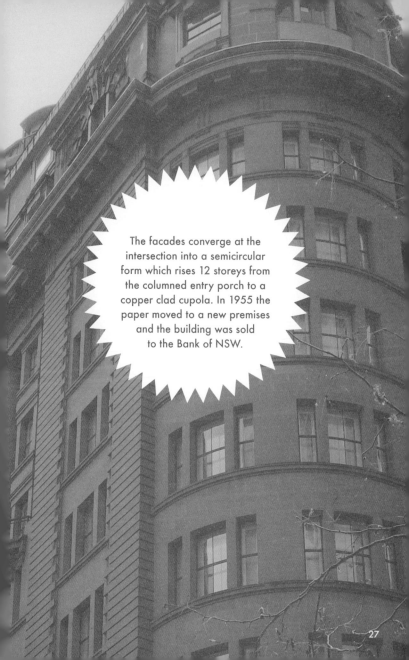

The facades converge at the intersection into a semicircular form which rises 12 storeys from the columned entry porch to a copper clad cupola. In 1955 the paper moved to a new premises and the building was sold to the Bank of NSW.

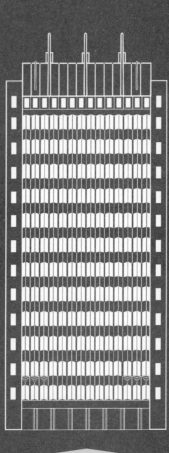

BRYANT HOUSE

Three years after the construction of the City Mutual headquarters Emil Sodersten was commissioned by the insurance company to design a building to be used as an investment property.

The architect once again produced a dramatic serrated facade treatment, although this time using brick. The effect is greatly enhanced by the framing of the surface on either side by flat planes, in addition to the richer textural qualities of the brick elements as opposed to the smooth-faced sandstone of the City Mutual Building. Raised above a polished granite plinth the fenestration extends 12 floors to a row of square recessed windows. A trio of vertical fins decorate the upper facade and continue over the roof parapet.

When completed Bryant House attracted a great deal of attention, not only for the exterior but for the lavish use of materials in the interior.

Whilst many of the original fittings have been removed or altered, the entry foyer and lift lobby retain Art Deco details including marble floors, decorative plaster elements and pressed metal ceilings.

✪ OF NOTE

St James Station / 1926 / George McRae

Designed by NSW Government Architect George McRae,
St James station opened in 1926 as part of the new eastern city line.
The Stripped Classical Elizabeth Street entrance (opposite David Jones)
features a stepped sandstone parapet with a decorative cartouche
indicating the 1926 construction date. Inside the entrance, sheltered
by a pressed-metal awning, is an original 1930s neon sign promoting
Chateau Tanunda brandy, a rare surviving example of pre-war
commercial advertising.

COMMONWEALTH BANK BUILDING

As the first fully steel framed structure in Sydney and the Commonwealth Bank's first national headquarters, this building holds an important place in the architectural and financial history of the city. The Commonwealth Bank of Australia was founded in 1911 as a commercial enterprise by the Labor Government under Prime Minister Andrew Fisher. Opening its first branch in Melbourne in 1912, it expanded via trade through post offices and, by 1913, had branches in all states. Locating its first head office in Sydney's CBD confirmed for many the city's role as Australia's financial capital.

An early example of Commercial Palazzo architecture in Sydney, the Martin Place facade is divided into four distinct sections via the use of differing materials and decorative elements. Smooth-faced trachyte clads the entry level with rusticated pilasters rising to a series of ornate cartouches. The remaining upper sections are clad in sandstone with the second and third sections featuring square pilasters capped with, respectively, shield motifs and Ionic capitals. The top section is punctuated by small recessed windows and is crowned by a broad cornice supported by multiple corbels.

Completed in 1916 the building was subject to two major subsequent additions; the first from 1929-1933 which extended the bank along Pitt Street and was architecturally sympathetic to the original building; the second, undertaken in 1965, extended the Martin Place facade and was designed in a late Stripped Classical manner.

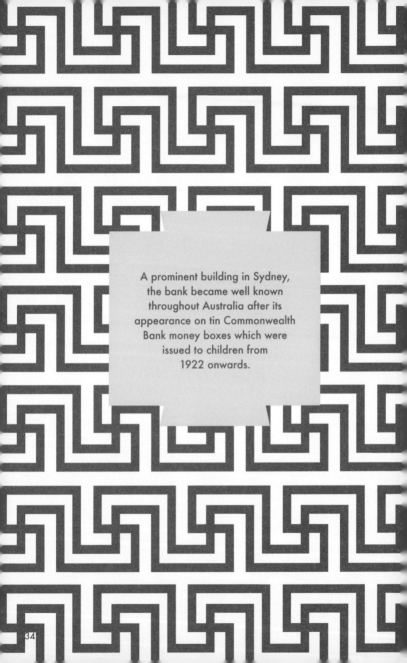

A prominent building in Sydney, the bank became well known throughout Australia after its appearance on tin Commonwealth Bank money boxes which were issued to children from 1922 onwards.

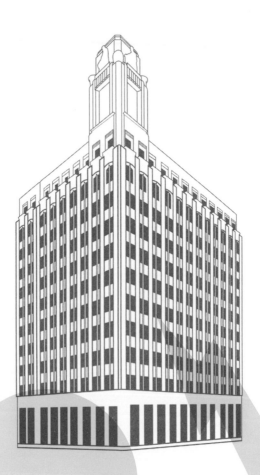

MLC BUILDING

By the mid-1930s those businesses that had managed to weather the worst years of the Great Depression were eager to move forward into a more prosperous era. The directors of the Mutual Life and Citizens Assurance Society demonstrated great optimism in the economic future by deciding to construct a new company headquarters on the site they had occupied since the late 1800s.

A design competition was held in 1936 and, from an initial list of 70 entries, the Melbourne firm of Bates, Smart & McCutcheon was chosen for the job. Founded in 1853 by Joseph Reed, it was one of Australia's most distinguished architectural firms and responsible for many of Melbourne's finest Victorian-era buildings, including the State Library and the 1880 Exhibition Buildings.

The Stripped Classical design of the MLC building comprises sandstone-clad facades raised upon a ground floor base of red granite. Sandstone piers, extending unbroken to the ninth floor, divide the fenestration into bays of twin rectangular windows, which are divided by rounded sandstone mullions. The spandrels are enamelled steel panels with horizontal fluted patterning. At the termination of the window bays, above the arched ninth floor windows, are a series of 'hollow and roll' or 'gorge' cornice forms. These are derived from ancient Egyptian architecture and reflect the fashion for using such motifs during the Art Deco period. Further motifs can be found on the corner tower in the form of papyrus shaped columns.

The tower also displays sculpted reliefs of a figure attempting to break a bundle of rods, under which is carved the company motto "Union is Strength".

The Sydney MLC project saw the beginning of a longstanding relationship between the company and Bates Smart & McCutcheon, with the firm being commissioned for numerous MLC office buildings around Australia throughout the 1950s.

✪ OF NOTE

State Savings Bank of New South Wales
48-50 Martin Place / 1928 / H E Ross & Rowe

Next to the MLC Building (across Castlereagh Street)
sits the former headquarters of the State Savings Bank.
Constructed in an imposing Beaux Arts style the building
was taken over by the Commonwealth Bank in 1931
and subsequently, along with the bank's Pitt Street
headquarters, became the subject for a tin money box
design. The red granite and pink terracotta tiled exterior
is matched by an elaborate interior that visitors are
encouraged to explore.

SUN BUILDING

The first in Sydney to be designed in the Skyscraper Gothic style, the former Sun building was also the last of the major newspaper-based offices to be constructed in the city. Sir Hugh Robert Denison came from a wealthy family whose fortune had been made in the tobacco industry. He founded Sun Newspapers Ltd in 1910 and rapidly expanded the business via the acquisition of various rival papers. The company purchased the lot between Elizabeth and Phillip Streets in 1921 in anticipation of the city council's extension plans for Martin Place, which would see the demolition of their existing offices.

The new headquarters, designed by Joseph Alexander Kethel, was officially opened on 15 October 1929 by the Governor of NSW, Sir Dudley de Chair. Kethel had previously designed numerous buildings for Sun Newspapers Ltd including a four-storey office for the Newcastle Sun, a regional paper acquired in 1918.

The Sun building represents a relatively restrained example of Skyscraper Gothic and includes idiosyncratic detailing such as the Tuscan column mullions dividing the first floor arch windows, a feature not usually associated with the style. Above a ground floor base of Uralla granite, the facade is clad in beige panels of Benedict stone (manufactured by the U.S based Benedict Stone Company by pouring a mix of stone dust and cement into moulds). Above the five ogee arch windows decorative mouldings launch piers and mullions upwards, terminating in a series of Gothic pinnacles. The roof is crowned with a sphere atop a small tower which, when the building was first opened, glistened with gold paint.

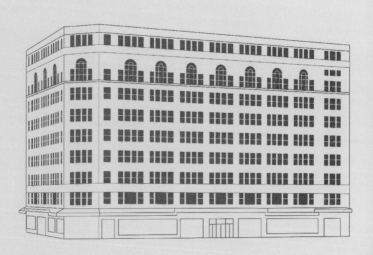

DAVID JONES BUILDINGS

Welsh merchant David Jones moved to Australia in 1835, opening his first store in 1838 on the corner of George and Barrack Streets with the intention of selling "the best and most exclusive goods". By the 1920s the now public company was being run by his grandson Charles Lloyd Jones who announced plans to construct a new store on a recently purchased block of land on Elizabeth Street.

Architectural firm Budden & Mackellar produced an elegant Stripped Classical building befitting the prestige of the client. Clad in sandstone, the facades express a lightness of form due to the steel frame structure that allowed for large rectangular windows divided by slim mullions. The building is divided into distinct sections, the first floor being differentiated by rusticated stone and the top by the use of multi-paned arched windows. The original copper-clad awning remains in place above street level and features decorative urns.

Sited diagonally opposite the 1927 building is the third David Jones store to be constructed in the city. Built to celebrate the company's 100th anniversary it was designed by the firm Mackeller & Partridge in the contemporary Streamline Moderne style. Contrasting with the classic angularity of the store opposite, the 1938 sandstone facade curves around the corner, emphasising the dynamic horizontality of the glazing bands.

External decoration is kept to a minimum with a ribbed awning and aluminium and glass grid panels above the street entrances. Originally six floors, four floors in the same style were added in 1951.

Both stores continue to be owned and operated by David Jones Ltd which is the oldest department store in the world still trading under its original name.

HYDE PARK
ANZAC MEMORIAL

It is a telling indication of the shock and grief felt following the bloody Anzac campaign on Gallipoli that fund raising for a memorial began on the first anniversary of the event (25 April 1916) while the war in Europe was still raging. In 1929 an official design competition was announced and local architect Charles Bruce Dellit produced the winning entry. Dellit had only recently established his private practice and the memorial would be the first of many projects that exhibited his pioneering Art Deco style throughout the 1930s.

Dominating the southern end of Hyde Park the memorial is constructed of concrete clad in pink granite panels. Square in form, the main block features square pilasters on each facade flanking large arched stained glass windows. The structure is crowned with a stepped, ziggurat-style roof.

Adorning the building both inside and out are numerous works by sculptor Raynor Hoff. Stone figures representing military personnel are perched atop the pilasters and roof corners whilst carved relief panels form a band around the structure. Above the east and west doors are ten-metre bronze friezes which depict the various activities and actions of the Australian Imperial Forces.

The interior of the memorial, however, holds the most dramatic of Hoff's pieces. Entering the memorial via ground level brings visitors into the marble-lined vestibule which in turn, leads to the Hall of Memory. Standing in the centre of the hall is 'Sacrifice', a bronze sculpture of a naked fallen soldier lying on a shield supported by three caryatids representing his mother, sister and wife. The naked figure was considered shocking at the time of its unveiling and precluded the installation of two further nudes intended for the exterior.

Opened on 24 November 1934
by Prince Henry, Duke of
Gloucester, the memorial is
considered to be Charles Bruce
Dellit's finest Art Deco work.

FOYS BUILDING

The Mark Foys Emporium building as it stands today is the result of major inter-war additions made to the original two-storey structure of 1909.

Irish immigrant Mark Foy ran a series of successful drapery stores in Melbourne during the 1870s and 80s, handing the business over to his two sons in 1882. In 1885, following a move to Sydney, Francis and Mark Foy Jr opened a store on Oxford Street. The business flourished and in 1909 the brothers constructed one of the grandest department stores the city had seen. Partly inspired by the pioneering Bon Marche department store in Paris (1852), the initial two-storey design was an interesting mix of early 20th century Chicagoesque and late 19th century Second Empire architectural styles. The 1928 extensions, which saw the construction of an additional four storeys, were designed in a similar manner.

Skirted by a large awning decorated with pressed metal soffits, the facades are clad with white glazed bricks, dramatically setting off the ornate yellow faience elements. Panels on the first level advertise goods available in the store while those on the second are adorned with floral motifs. Rising above a simple cornice with corbels, the 1928 facade features square pilasters with Corinthian capitals dividing wide window bays. The upper level, adorned with green Solomonic column mullions, is topped on the Liverpool Street elevation by ornate gabled parapets flanked by two prominent mansard roofed towers.

Highly profitable until well after World War 2, Foy's struggled throughout the 1960s and 70s before closing the store in 1983. The building is now occupied by the NSW State Courts.

PLAZA THEATRE

Throughout the 1920s and 30s cinemas, or picture palaces as they were known in the UK and Australia, were often designed in a style that represented the escapist glamour displayed on the screens within. The 2000 seat Plaza Theatre, with its Spanish Baroque detailing, was certainly no exception.

Built for the Hoyts Group the theatre is constructed of brick with a textured render finish and precast concrete decoration. The George Street facade is chamfered on both sides and dominated by a highly ornate central arrangement of pilasters and arched windows. The four pilasters are decorated with geometric relief patterns and topped by Corinthian capitals. Three bays of multi-paned windows are divided by ornate spandrels and are set back from balustraded balconettes. The pilasters rise to individual cornices which further extend to corresponding spiral urns sitting atop the roof parapet.

The years following the end of World War 2 saw a decline in cinema attendance, accelerated by the introduction of television to Australian cities in 1956. Although the Plaza ceased to function as a cinema in 1977, it escaped the terminal fate of many other city theatres through the utilisation of the venue for various entertainment purposes over the years. Initially converted to a skating rink, the auditorium has also been used as a live concert venue and restaurant. A McDonald's restaurant has occupied the foyer since 1977, the only part of the theatre that still retains its original interior elements including roof beams and decorative Spanish motifs.

✪ OF NOTE

Bebarfalds / 1929 / Kent & Massie

Furniture and homewares retailer Bebarfalds occupied the prestigious site opposite Sydney Town Hall (cnr George and Park Streets) from 1894. The building that exists today was constructed in 1929, initially to eight levels. The Stripped Classical design sits on a rusticated base and features a simple square fenestration treatment with decorative spandrel panels on the seventh floor. The second floor was originally used for display rooms including an entire fully furnished, six room Spanish Bungalow style home. Two additional floors were added in 1967, shortly before a takeover by Ajax Insurance Ltd.

METROPOLITAN WATER, SEWERAGE & DRAINAGE BOARD BUILDING

With the 1939 Metropolitan Water Sewerage & Drainage Board building, architects Budden & Mackey not only provided a modern headquarters for the organisation but gave Sydney what is now considered one of the city's finest and most exquisitely detailed Art Deco structures.

The Government entity now known as Sydney Water was formed in 1888, initially occupying offices at Circular Quay. In 1890 the department moved to Pitt Street where it remained throughout various office renovations and expansions until a 2009 move to Parramatta. The 1939 building dramatically demonstrates the stylistic development of the Art Deco architectural movement from the vertical angularity of the 1920s to the horizontal streamlined forms of the late 1930s. Facade elements are clearly articulated by the use of contrasting materials beginning with a ground-level base of red granite cladding framing a colonnade of black granite piers. Wide horizontal bronze banding and yellow faience mullions frame the upper level bronze windows, rounding the corner in a smooth transition.

The main entrance is marked by four vertical faience clad fins which extend up the height of the facade, forming three bays of smaller bronze windows. Three bas relief panels, sculpted by Stanley Hammond, sit above the entrance and depict mankind's dependence upon water. After the departure of Sydney Water the interior was refurbished for use as a luxury hotel, although many of the original materials and elements have been retained.

GOWINGS

GOWINGS BUILDING

On 29 January 2006, after years of declining sales, the Gowings store on George Street closed its doors for the last time. Established in 1868 by John Gowing and his brother Preston, the menswear retailer was a deeply entrenched Sydney institution with stores throughout the city and suburbs. One of the company's post-war advertising slogans, "Gone to Gowings", had even made its way into the local vernacular as meaning a person or thing was missing or irretrievably lost.

Designed in the Commercial Palazzo style, the building on the corner of George and Market Streets was purpose-built for Gowings, becoming their flagship CBD store. Clad in sandstone, the 12 storey structure presents two street facades flanking a chamfered corner. The first and second floors are rusticated with squared pilasters extending to an entablature and cornice. The restrained mid-section is composed of clearly articulated sandstone blocks punctuated by sash windows and separated from the upper two levels by a simple cornice form. Decorative details of the lower levels are repeated at the top section with the addition of corbelled window ledges and ornate pilaster capitals.

Since the departure of Gowings the building's interior has been extensively refurbished and is now home to a major UK based fashion retailer and luxury hotel. The Gowings signage adorning the facades has also been restored and now advertises an upscale bar and grill restaurant in the building.

⭐ OF NOTE

State Theatre / 1929 / Henry E. White

Next door to Gowings is the spectacular State Theatre. Completed just before the Great Depression, the building is a flamboyant showcase of theatrical architectural and decorative styles.

The Gothic-inspired facade, with its spiral mullion forms and gargoyles, seems positively Spartan compared to the lavish interiors. From the spectacular entrance to the domed Baroque Grand Assembly, leading into the splendid 2000 seat auditorium, the theatre is an overwhelming sensory experience.

DYMOCKS BUILDING

Beginning in 1879 with a small store on Market Street, by the 1890s Dymocks Booksellers claimed to be "the largest book shop in the world, holding upwards of one million books". The founder, William Dymock, died in 1900 aged just 39 and the business was subsequently run by his sister, Marjory, and her husband John Forsyth. At the time the bookstore was operating out of a leased shop that was part of the Royal Hotel building on George Street, an arrangement that continued into the 1920s. By 1922 the continuing success of the business enabled the Forsyth family to purchase the Royal Hotel site with the intention of constructing a flagship bookstore and shopping arcade.

Construction commenced in 1926 but wasn't completed until 1932 due to financial difficulties caused by the Great Depression. The 11 storey building, with its clearly divided facade sections, is an interesting example of the Commercial Palazzo style. Clad in unusual grey 'granite' terracotta, the lower levels form a classic base of vertical forms including square Doric pilasters terminating at a simple entablature with dentilled cornice. The middle section is composed of three distinct bays, the central bay being clad in a Chicagoesque curtain wall of bronze spandrels and mullions. The flanking bays are punctuated with simple unadorned rectangular windows with the exception of corbelled balconies on the tenth floor. A decorative cartouche sits atop the central facade, above which sits the top level crowned by an elaborate entablature.

'The Block',
as the building is also known,
refers to the shopping arcade above
the Dymocks store, occupied by various
small businesses over the years. Accessed
via the central street entrance, the interiors
are largely original and include
terrazzo floors, silky oak
shopfronts and leadlight
elements.

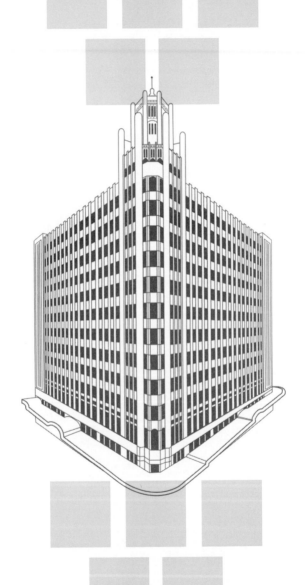

GRACE BUILDING

The Grace brothers, Albert Edward and Joseph Neal, kicked off their retail enterprise in the 1880s by selling goods door to door throughout Sydney. By the 1920s the firm now known as Grace Bros Ltd was firmly entrenched as one of the city's major retailers and the brothers were looking to construct a new headquarters. Reasoning that the imminent opening of the Sydney Harbour Bridge would direct increasing pedestrian traffic along York and Clarence Streets, a site was purchased in the area in 1926.

Architects Morrow and Gordon were commissioned to design the building, producing a spectacular Skyscraper Gothic structure heavily influenced by the Tribune Tower in Chicago (1925). Clad in cream faience tiles, the soaring verticality of the facades is emphasised by the expressed mullion forms used to divide the fenestration. First floor windows are topped by Gothic arched tracery spandrels highlighted with green panels. The corner features four main pilasters rising beyond the 12th floor to form a buttressed tower.

Opened by Lord Mayor Alderman ES Marks on 3 July, 1930 the building drew immediate praise for its dramatic appearance and modern amenities including the light-filled, well-ventilated offices and high-speed lifts. Utilising the first two levels as a department store, the remaining floors were to be leased out as office space. This proved difficult, however, due to the economic effects of the Great Depression and failure of increased traffic to the area to materialise as previously envisioned.

In 1942 the Australian Government requisitioned the building for use by various Commonwealth Departments, retaining it until well after 1945. After compensating Grace Bros Ltd for the loss of the building in 1953, various government departments worked out of the premises until it was sold to a private hotel group in 1995.

✪ OF NOTE

Asbestos House / 1929 / Robertson & Marks

Sited on the corner of York and Barrack Streets is the former
headquarters of building materials firm James Hardie.
Grey granite tiles clad the first two levels with the remaining
upper floors finished in rendered masonry. The facades are
given a strong sense of verticality with continuous mullion
forms intersecting pale green spandrels. The Stripped Classical
form displays subtle Egyptian inspired Art Deco motifs on the
front entrance and roof cornice.

AWA TOWER

For much of the 20th century Amalgamated Wireless (Australasia) Ltd operated as Australia's largest electronics manufacturer and broadcaster. The company was directly involved in many early communication milestones including receiving the first radio broadcast from the UK to Australia (1918) and transmitting the first newsreel pictures from Sydney to London (1930).

Constructed in 1939 as a new headquarters, AWA Tower clearly communicated the Art Deco movement's integration of architecture and technology. Clad in brick, the facade presents a soaring skyscraper aesthetic with a central six window bay rising beyond narrower flanking bays. The facade steps back to form the base for the communications tower which, at 46 metres on top of the main structure's 55-metres, made AWA Tower the tallest building in Sydney until the 1960s. The tower itself was partly modelled on the Funkturm Berlin (Berlin Radio Tower), constructed in 1926 for the Third Great German Radio Exhibition.

Decoration is minimal with the AWA logo sitting below the tower and a mosaic tiled sculpture of the winged horse 'Pegasus'on the parapet. The entrance level is faced with trachyte which, in its geometric shapes, reflects the termination form of the upper floors. The glass awning with decorative waterfall motifs is a later addition. The entry foyer and lift lobby remain in original decorative form, faced with Wombeyan marble with streamlined details.

AWA didn't survive
into the 21st century.
It was absorbed into
the Jupiter Group
which currently
owns the building.

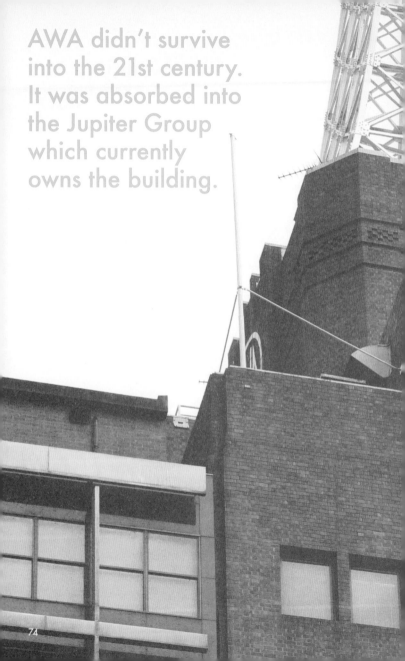

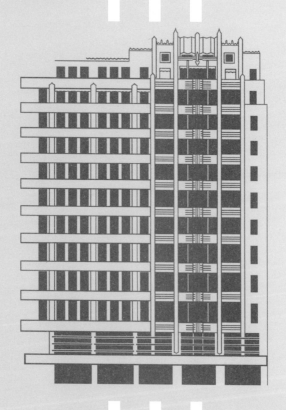

RAILWAY HOUSE

Sydney's first suburban train line opened on 26 September 1855, linking the city to Parramatta via four stations. The network rapidly expanded and by 1926 was fully electrified. With the opening of Sydney Harbour Bridge in 1932 the existing North Shore Line was linked to the CBD by the newly constructed Wynyard and Town Hall underground stations. Wynyard station was subsequently chosen as the site for the New South Wales State Railways administrative headquarters, with construction beginning in 1934.

Originally conceived as a dominant central tower flanked by horizontal wings, the final asymmetrical design was well received. It possesses a modern aesthetic with subtle yet dynamic Art Deco detailing. Unbroken horizontal spandrel bands run across the main block, dividing the bronze framed windows into Modernist strips. The tower section rises in three bays created by four vertical fins, terminating in a stepped Deco skyscraper manner at the top. The tower spandrels are decorated with ornate central panels and horizontal line forms. The entire facade above ground level is clad in green faience tiles, chosen to match the colour of contemporary train carriages and a shade subsequently used for a period on all of Sydney's public transport including its ferries. Entered via Railway House, Wynyard station retains many original 1930s fittings including escalators with timber tread and veneer panelling manufactured by the Otis Company.

Shortly after opening, Railway House was awarded the Royal Australian Institute of Architects Sulman Award (1935) followed by a Royal Institute of British Architects Medal in 1939.

COMMERCIAL BANKING & BANK OF NSW BUILDINGS

Two of Australia's earliest financial institutions, the Commercial Banking Company of Sydney (est. 1834) and the Bank of NSW (est. 1817) had both occupied the block on George Street since the 1850s. Presenting an image of prosperity and confidence to the public was important in the years following the First World War and the CBC decided to achieve this by constructing a grand new headquarters at 343 George Street. A Commercial Palazzo-style building with clear classic motifs, the upper sandstone-clad levels sit above a base of rusticated stone. The George Street entrance is highlighted by four trachyte columns with Ionic capitals supporting an entablature engraved with the company name. Tall bronze-framed arch windows skirt the ground level whilst the sandstone facades are punctuated with bays of rectangular casement windows.

Abutting the CBC building is the equally impressive 1932 Bank of NSW. Constructed as a direct response to their business rival, the bank directed architects Robertson & Marks to design a building that matched the height and floor articulation of the neighbouring structure. Designed in a decoratively more restrained style, the George Street facade is dominated by the enormous arched entrance faced with grey rusticated stone. Within the arch the bank's coat of arms sits atop an entablature supported by red granite columns.

THE COMMERCIAL BANKING

✪ OF NOTE

Challis House / 1938 / Hennessey & Hennessey

Across from the bank buildings, on Martin Place,
is an interesting redevelopment of an early 20th century
structure. Originally constructed in 1907 for Sydney
University, Challis House was given an entirely new facade
in 1938. Named after university benefactor John Henry
Challis (1806-1880) the building was updated with a
severe Stripped Classical design with Art Deco detailing.
The main entrance is framed by red granite, inside which
are bronze doors topped by a transom window displaying
the Sydney University crest and motto.

OMPANY OF SYDNEY LIMITED

A deliberate act of one upmanship between corporate rivals, the Bank of NSW building was widely criticised by contemporary architects and academics as clashing aesthetically with its neighbour and of cheekily "making its entrance look like the entrance to both buildings".

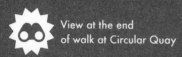
View at the end
of walk at Circular Quay

SYDNEY HARBOUR BRIDGE

Nicknamed the "Coathanger" by locals, the Sydney Harbour Bridge is, along with the Opera House, the most recognisable built symbol of the city.

Plans to link the northern and southern shores of Sydney Harbour were first proposed by convict architect Francis Greenway in 1815. Many other suggestions were put forward throughout the 19th century but it wasn't until after the First World War that serious action was taken to design and construct a bridge. John Bradfield had been appointed Chief Engineer of Sydney Harbour Bridge and Metropolitan Railway Construction in 1914 and, following the war, began to develop ideas for a suitable structure. Initially favouring a cantilever design, Bradfield and his team eventually decided that a single arched bridge would be more suitable as it was both cheaper and offered more structural rigidity. Inspired by the Hells Gate Bridge in New York City (1916) the winning design, submitted via a 1923 tendering process, was produced by UK engineering firm Dorman Long and Company Ltd. Construction began in 1924 and was completed in January 1932 at a total cost of AU£6.25 million.

Stretching between Millers Point at the southern end and Milsons Point at the north, the main arch is composed of grey painted steel trusses and joists. The large towers at the each end of the span are concrete clad in granite quarried from Moruya, NSW. Although abutment structures at their bases support the arch loads, the towers themselves were designed for purely aesthetic reasons, serving no engineering purpose.

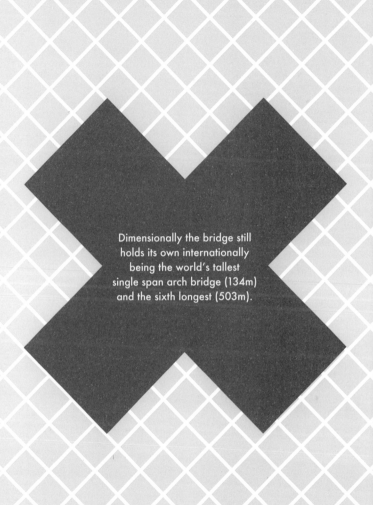

Dimensionally the bridge still holds its own internationally being the world's tallest single span arch bridge (134m) and the sixth longest (503m).

GEORGE RAYNOR HOFF

(1894 – 1937)

The son of a woodcarver and stonemason, George Raynor Hoff was born on the Isle of Man on 27 November 1894. Assisting his father on architectural projects from an early age, he went on to study drawing and design at Nottingham School of Art from 1910 to 1915. He enlisted in the British Army in 1915, was sent to France the following year and fought in the trenches before being transferred to a topographical survey unit. These experiences no doubt left an indelible mark on his psyche, reflected in the powerful pieces he later created for various war memorial projects.

After the war Hoff studied at the Royal College of Art under sculptor Francis Derwent Wood and in 1921 travelled to Rome on a scholarship. A meeting with Australian architect Hardy Wilson in Naples sparked a series of events that led to the young artist being appointed director of sculpture and drawing at East Sydney Technical College in May, 1923.

An energetic artist and administrator, Hoff sought to raise the profile of sculpture in Australia through the exhibition and promotion not only of his own work but that of his students.

Sculpting works in all scales (including numerous medal designs for various arts and industry awards) his most significant contributions to the medium were the large publicly visible pieces, especially those commissioned for war memorials.

Beginning with three bronze relief panels for the Dubbo Memorial (1925), Hoff was subsequently commissioned to design marble reliefs and bronze statues for the National War Memorial in Adelaide (1930) followed by extensive panels and sculptures for the Hyde Park ANZAC Memorial (1934). Although his artistic inspirations were broad, ranging from classical Graeco-Roman to Art Deco, the figures represented in these pieces appear neither excessively heroic nor superficially stylised; Hoff instead managed to embed in them a sense of nobility and humanity whilst still communicating the tragedy of the events depicted.

The dramatic centrepiece of the Hyde Park Memorial, 'Sacrifice', is a powerful symbol of the Great War's young victims, as truly understood and represented by Hoff, the veteran and artist.

Hoff died in 1937 of pancreatitis at the age of just 42.

Although now widely considered the most important sculptor working in Sydney during the inter-war years, most Australians are unknowingly aware of his work through the Holden car company. Designed by Hoff in 1928 the "lion and stone" logo, although altered slightly over the years, remains the corporate symbol of the firm.

INTER-WAR TIMELINE
1914-1939

1914 Outbreak of the First World War. Australia pledges full support to Britain after she declares war on Germany in August.

1915 The Gallipoli campaign begins with the landing of the Australian Imperial Forces (AIF) on Anzac Cove on 25 April.

1916 Taronga Zoo opens on 7 October. Taronga is an indigenous word meaning 'beautiful view'.

1918 The First World War ends with an armistace declared on 11 November, by which time over 60,000 Australian soldiers have been killed.

1921 Inaugural Archibald Prize (administered by trustees of the Art Gallery of NSW) is won by William McInnes for a portrait of architect H. Desbrowe Annear. Annear (1865-1933) was instrumental in the development of the Arts and Craft movement in Australia.

1922 Independent children's charity the Smith Family is founded in Sydney by five businessmen.

1923 First official radio station begins broadcasting in Sydney. Initially known as 2SB it is now 702 ABC Sydney, the flagship station in the ABC local radio network.

1924 First regular commercial flights begin operating from Sydney airport (Mascot).

1929 The Great Depression hits. Continuing construction of Sydney Harbour Bridge, begun in 1923, alleviates to some extent the unemployment crisis.

1932 The official opening of Sydney Harbour Bridge is famously disrupted by Francis De Groot, a member of right-wing royalist group the 'New Guard'. De Groot, mounted on horseback and wearing a military uniform, rides up and slashes the ceremonial opening ribbon with his sword.

1935 Luna Park, constructed at the foot of Sydney Harbour Bridge, opens 4 October.

1938 Sydney hosts the third British Empire Games from 5-12 February to coincide with Sydney's sesqui-centenary (150 years since the foundation of British settlement in Australia).

1939 Australia follows Britain in the declaration of war on Germany.

Art Deco: Taking its name from the 1925 Exposition Internationale des Arts Décoratifs et Industriels Modernes, the Art Deco style used vibrant colour and geometric shapes to express the speed and movement of industry and the Machine Age

Balconette: A false balcony created by a stone balustrade or cast iron railing framing the lower section of an upper floor window

Baroque: Elaborate, overly ornate decorative style originating in 17th century Italy

Buttress A structure of masonry or brick used to provide lateral support to a wall

Chamfered: A transitional edge between two facades of a building, usually a 45° angle

Chicagoesque: A style resulting from pioneering developments in the U.S (particularly Chicago) relating to steel frame engineering which enabled architects to design facades that expressed the inner structure, thereby creating larger window apertures. A precursor to the light curtain wall designs of the 1950s

Colonnade: A series of columns supporting an entablature

Commercial Palazzo: A style that utilized the form and proportions of Italian Renaissance palaces for late 19th and early 20th century commercial buildings

Coping: The capping or covering of a wall

Corinthian: One of the five classical orders, characterized by acanthus leaves decorating the capitals

Cornice: A continuous horizontal moulding crowning a building or aperture

Dentil: A small block used in repetition as a decorative feature on a cornice

Doric: One of the five classical orders, characterised by a plain square capital

Entablature: The structure above the capital comprising architrave, frieze and cornice

Facade: An exterior side of a building, often referring to the front

Faience: Glazed terracotta tiles used for architectural cladding

Federation Style:
Encompassing various revival styles popular in England around 1890-1915 (including Queen Anne and Edwardian) Federation architecture utilised, amongst other elements, extensive brickwork and decorative roof features

Fenestration: The arrangement and design of windows in a building

Frieze: The central component of the entablature, often decorated with a relief design

Gable: The triangular part of a wall between the sloping faces of a pitched roof

Ionic: One of the five classical orders, characterised by a scroll-like ornament decorating the capital and often fluted shaft

Loggia: A covered exterior gallery enclosed on one side by arcades or colonnades.

Mansard: French style four-sided roof

Mullion: A vertical form dividing a window

Parapet: A vertical extension of the facade wall at the edge of a roof

Pediment: A classical triangular shaped structure placed above the entablature of a building

Pier: An upright element or section providing structural support

Pilasters: A column feature projecting from the face of a wall (as opposed to a freestanding column)

Portico: A porch extending from the main body of a building

Quoin: Cornerstones of a wall, often rusticated.

Rustication: A masonry technique used to accentuate the joins between stone blocks. The face of each block is also often given a rough or patterned finish to further delineate each stone

Second Empire: Late 19th/early 20th century architecture inspired by that of the 2nd French Empire (1852 to 1870). Includes features such as Classic motifs, Baroque detailing and Mansard roofs.

Skyscraper Gothic: A Neo-Gothic style that applied soaring, vertical cathedral-like forms to skyscraper architecture.

Soffits: The underside of an architectural structure such as an awning or balcony

Solomonic column: A column with a spiral or twisting shaft

Spandrel: The space between the top of a window and the sill of the window in the storey above

Streamline Moderne: A late Art Deco style that emphasised horizontal lines and curved forms relating to vehicular movement

Stripped Classical: Inter-war architecture presenting classic architectural forms devoid of most or all ornamentation

Terrazzo: A flooring material composed of chips of marble, quartz, granite or glass, mixed with a binder and applied to the surface

Voussoir: A wedge-shaped element that forms part of an arch

Ziggurat: A terraced step pyramid form associated with ancient Middle Eastern architecture

THE WALK

The Footpath Guide to Inter-War architecture in Sydney takes approximately two hours to complete.